A Partridge in a Pear Tree

The Twelve Days of Christmas

Michele Jeanmarie

Illustrated by Mochu Shobaru

A Partridge in a Pear Tree

The Twelve Days of Christmas

by

Michele Jeanmarie

(A Children's Theatre)

This is a work of fiction. All of the characters, names, incidents, organizations, and dialogue in this novel are either the products of the author's imagination or are used fictitiously.

Archway Publishing
1663 Liberty Drive
Bloomington, IN 47403
www.archwaypublishing.com
844-669-3957

Because of the dynamic nature of the Internet, any web addresses or links contained in this book may have changed since publication and may no longer be valid. The views expressed in this work are solely those of the author and do not necessarily reflect the views of the publisher, and the publisher hereby disclaims any responsibility for them.

Interior Image Credit: Mochu Shobaru

ISBN: 978-1-6657-4756-1 (sc)
978-1-6657-4757-8 (e)

Library of Congress Control Number: 2023914084

Archway Publishing rev. date: 08/04/2023

A Partridge in a Pear Tree

The Twelve Days of Christmas

Introduction

"Ugh! When will we learn to be compassionate and kind and tolerant? When did we get so divided?" Chela mused.

Narrator:

Once upon a time, long, long time ago, around the 1560s, there was a man of royalty, who went by the name of King Henry VIII. As a king and royal, he is to continue the monarchy. This could only be achieved through marriage, through a male heir, a boy. So, as a young adult, King Henry VIII married, hopeful he would get a male heir. He got three! Sadly, they all died in childbirth, or shortly thereafter. King Henry VIII grew frustrated after several attempts. The weight of the monarchy laid on his head. He decided it was time to find another prospect. But alas! He was not allowed to have another prospect. The Vatican, Rome, home to the pope, said he could not!

"But I am king!" He bellowed.

Narrator:

Henry VIII decided to oust every member associated with Rome. He expelled all those affiliated with Rome from his palace. Known as Catholics, they became afraid of him, very afraid. They left. Some set sail. Some hid. It is this group that stayed in hiding that yearned for what was lost, their faith, their community.

"How can we rebuild our community?" They mused.

They devised a plan.

"We must think of something."

They do! The "Twelve Days of Christmas," would be written as a song and was going to be the vehicle to impart knowledge, to teach the faith, to teach the community. This song will be sung every year during the Christmas season. It would embed messages and symbolisms and doctrines to teach the Catholic faith. They made a long list and decided that twelve was the perfect number.

One rationalizes, "Well, there are twelve apostles. The song will end with them, the creed, 'The Apostles Creed.'"

Another adds, "Beginning on December 25 and ending on the epiphany makes twelve days of Christmas."

Says another, "But it can also begin twelve days before Christmas, which is Advent."

And another, "The song will be called the Twelve Days of Christmas. It would be jubilant and festive and pretty catchy. There will be repetition, and it'll be sung every year of the Christmas season."

They commence:

"A Partridge in a Pear Tree will represent the one and only Jesus Christ," explains one. "The partridge is a bird. It appears in the pear tree. Pear is a fruit that promotes birth, fertility, life. Life encourages life, and so his followers, that is, we, are encouraged to promote life."

On The 1st day of Christmas, my true love sent to me:

"A Partridge in a Pear Tree."

They continue, "The two turtle doves refer to the Old Testament and the New Testament. The Old Testament is the first half of the good book, the Bible. It teaches us the early religion of the Jewish people. It sheds light on the old…"

"And the New Testament sheds light on the new. Jesus, the Partridge in the pear tree, came to manifest what is in the old, the Old Testament."

On the 2nd day of Christmas, my true love sent to me:

Two turtle doves, and a

"A Partridge in a Pear Tree."

"Three. Now comes three."

"Shall we use French hens?" asks another.

"The three French hens refer to faith, hope and love," carries on one.

Narrator: Faith, hope, and love are known as the Theological virtues. They are known as Theological virtues because "theo" is anything that comes from God and "logo" is the Word of God. He explains that like a muscle, theological virtues need to become part of one's daily regime, with continuous use, practice, and repetition exercises.

"Such was not the case with King Henry VIII," chastises one. "He split his own community."

"Some stayed with him," another observes.

And another, "others left."

On the 3rd day of Christmas, my true love sent to me:

Three French hens,

Two turtle doves, and a

"A Partridge in a Pear Tree."

"Lovely," exclaims one. "The four calling birds refer to the Gospels of Matthew, Mark, Luke and John.

"Matthew, Mark, Luke and John each have their own symbols," states one, furrowing his brows, as he tries to jot something down. "Help me out, here."

"St. Matthew is always shown as a divine man. St. Mark, is always shown as a winged lion," rustling through the Bible, he adds, "St. Luke is always shown as a winged ox, and St. John, is always shown as a rising eagle."

"These four walked with Jesus, the partridge in the pear tree, and were to recount all they could in writing to spread the good Word, whilst growing the community," a third one punctuates.

On the 4th day of Christmas, my true love sent to me:

Four calling birds,

Three French hens,

Two turtle doves, and a

"A Partridge in a Pear Tree."

Matthew   Mark   John   Luke

"Brilliant, coming along well," ascents one.

The other resumes, "The five golden rings refer to the Pentateuch, the first five books in the Old Testament. They are Genesis, Exodus, Leviticus, Numbers and Deuteronomy."

Says one, "the Pentateuch is also known as the Torah by the Jewish people."

"Genesis is about Creation, the Garden of Eden and our very first parents, Adam and Eve, and how they got expelled from their first home. Exodus narrates the story of the Jewish people leaving Egypt, where they were enslaved. Leviticus involves all the Jewish Rules," delineates one.

"Rules establish order, a key component necessary to establish relationships and trust," interrupts another.

"The other resumes, "Numbers made sure census was kept, and Deuteronomy is Moses' own words of God's rules."

On the 5th day of Christmas, my true love sent to me:

FIVE golden rings,

Four calling birds,

Three French hens,

Two turtle doves, and a

"A Partridge in a Pear Tree."

The Pentateuch

Genesis

Exodus

Numbers

Leviticus

Deuteronomy

"Just wonderful," admires one. "Next is number six!"

"What can we use?" he asks. He springs up, "Geese!"

"The six geese-a-laying refers to the six days of Creation."

The small group of men, in hiding, decided to simply quote their Bible. It reads,

"From darkness, light was created. Darkness was called 'night,' and light was called 'day.'

The first day.

Through the middle of the waters, a vault was created. The vault above was called heaven.

The second day.

The water below heaven came together as one mass. Dry land appeared, called earth, and the remaining water was the sea. From earth, vegetation was produced: seed-bearing plants and fruit-bearing trees, with their seed inside, each corresponding to its own species.

The third day.

Back in heaven, two great lights were created: one was to govern the day and the lesser one was to govern the night and the stars. These lights were to shine on earth to mark festivals, days, and years.

The fourth day.

From the waters, a swarm of living creatures were created, sea-monsters and creatures that glide and teem in their waters in their own species. Winged creatures, also in their own species, were created to wing their way above the earth across the vault of heaven.

The fifth day.

On the earth, every kind of living species was created: cattle in their own species, creeping things in their own species and wild animals in their own species. Finally, in his own image, in his own likeness, he made man and made him masters of the fish of the sea, the birds of heaven, the cattle, all the wild animals and all the creatures that creep along the ground.

The sixth day.

It took God six days to create all of this. He blessed the seventh day holy, because on that day he rested after all his work of creating.

The seventh day."

They all step back and are satisfied.

On the 6th day of Christmas, my true love sent to me:

Six geese-a-laying,

FIVE golden rings,

Four calling birds,

Three French hens,

Two turtle doves, and a

"A Partridge in a Pear Tree."

"We come to number seven," perseveres one.

"Seven!"

"Seven swans. We'll use swans in this verse. There are seven gifts of the Holy Spirit," contributes another. "The Seven Gifts of the Holy Spirit," he presses on, "are reminders of what is pleasing, pure, and perfect. The Holy Spirit is known as the Advocate, who helps and speaks on behalf of the self. Knowing divisions…" (voice trails)

Flips one, "as we are now in the middle of it…," (his voice trailing)

He persists and begins again, "Knowing divisions would distance his children from him, God sent the Holy Spirit with these gifts to help us, to advocate and speak on our behalf. The Holy Spirit is often seen as a dove."

Flippantly says the one again, "We cannot use 'dove,' as they all know what a dove means to us."

"Then we shall use 'geese.'" Retorted the one. "Let us simply use our Bible. Yes? Let us explain each one."

The seven gifts of the Holy Spirit are:

Wisdom: makes us see God in all things
and persons and seek him above all things.

Understanding: helps us understand
the Word of God and his doctrines.

Counsel: we are to make the solution
God would make for the good of all.

Fortitude: helps us overcome difficulties with faith.

Knowledge: helps us see the world from God's perspective.

Piety: trust in God.

Fear of God: turn away from sin and choose what is pleasing to him.

"Excellent," they congratulate each other.

On the 7th day of Christmas, my true love sent to me:

Seven swans-a-swimming,

Six geese-a-laying,

FIVE golden rings,

Four calling birds,

Three French hens,

Two turtle doves, and a

"A Partridge in a Pear Tree."

Abiding in the spirit, the group of men loiter on, "Eight!"

"Eight maids, we shall use. We have eight Beatitudes."

Another, "Nothing like King Henry VIII."

Another repudiates, "He knows them. He chooses not to abide in them."

"Shall we choose to copy them from Galatians?" asks one.

"Yes," consents one. "I have them here. Love, joy, peace, patience, kindness, goodness, faithfulness, gentleness and self-control refer to the Fruits of the Holy Spirit."

"Why are they called fruits?" wonders one.

The other replied, "They are called fruits, because like fruits provide nourishment for the body, these fruits provide nourishment for the soul."

One cajoles, "The King could use a dosage of some right now."

On the 8th day of Christmas, my true love sent to me:

Eight maids a-milking,

Seven swans-a-swimming,

Six geese-a-laying,

FIVE golden rings,

Four calling birds,

Three French hens,

Two turtle doves, and a

"A Partridge in a Pear Tree."

Blessed are the poor in spirit :
for theirs is the kingdom of heaven.
Blessed are the meek: for they shall possess the land.
Blessed are they who mourn:
for they shall be comforted.
Blessed are they that hunger and thirst after justice :
for they shall have their fill.
Blessed are the merciful:
for they shall obtain mercy.
Blessed are the clean of heart:
for they shall see God.
Blessed are the peacemakers:
for they shall be called the children of God.
Blessed are they that suffer
persecution for justice' sake,
for theirs is the kingdom of heaven.

"Nine!"

"Nine, it is" agrees one.

"What are we to use?"

"Nine ladies! They shall be leaping."

"Stupendous!"

"Which doctrine has nine elements in it?" asks one.

"The nine fruits of the Holy Spirit," he repeats. "They are love, joy, peace, patience, kindness, goodness, faithfulness, gentleness and self-control. Just as fruits provide nourishment to the body, these fruits provide nourishment for the soul."

"Let me," he writes.

On the 9th day of Christmas, my true love sent to me:

Nine ladies leaping,

Eight maids a-milking,

Seven swans-a-swimming,

Six geese-a-laying,

FIVE golden rings,

Four calling birds,

Three French hens,

Two turtle doves, and a

"A Partridge in a Pear Tree."

Love
Joy
Patience
Faithfulness
Peace
Self-Control
Kindness
Goodness
Gentleness

"Whew," they keep on.

"Ten! We are now at ten."

"Shall we use lords, his lords?" inquires one.

"We shall use Lords leaping to the news of the Ten Commandments."

As with the creation story, the three men decided to copy their Bible.

1. I am the Lord your God; thou shall not have strange gods before Me.

2. Thou shall not take the Name of the Lord your God in vain.

3. Remember to keep holy the Lord's day.

4. Honor thy father and thy mother.

5. Thou shall not kill.

6. Thou shall not commit adultery.

7. Thou shall not steal.

8. Thou shall not bear false witness against thy neighbour.

9. Thou shall not covet thy neighbour's wife.

10. Thou shall not covet thy neighbour's goods.

On the 10th day of Christmas, my true love sent to me:

Ten Lords-a-leaping,

Nine ladies leaping,

Eight maids a-milking,

Seven swans-a-swimming,

Six geese-a-laying,

FIVE golden rings,

Four calling birds,

Three French hens,

Two turtle doves, and a

"A Partridge in a Pear Tree."

THE 10 Commandments

1. I am the Lord thy God, thou shalt have no other gods before me.

2. You shall make no idols.

3. Thou shalt not take the name of the Lord thy God in vain.

4. Remember the Sabbath Day to keep holy.

5. Honor thy father and thy mother.

6. Thou shalt not kill.

7. Thou shalt not commit adultery.

8. Thou shalt not steal.

9. Thou shalt not bear false witness.

10. Thou shalt not covet.

"Now, we've come to eleven!"

"What shall we use that fits into the song?"

"Pipers!" declares one. "Eleven pipers."

"Eleven pipers for the eleven apostles."

"But there were twelve." Contradicts one.

"We are going to use eleven, because Judas had taken his own life. There were only eleven when Jesus resurrected. So, we shall use eleven, as there were only eleven to whom he appeared after his resurrection."

"There will be some explaining to do." Demands one.

"So shall there be. In fact, better."

"Let us list them," as one prepares,

1. Simon, also known as Peter,

2. and his brother Andrew;

3. James son of Zebedee,

4. and his brother John;

5. Philip and

6. Bartholomew;

7. Thomas and

8. Matthew the tax collector;

9. James son of Alphaeus, and

10. Thaddaeus;

11. Simon the Cananaean.

On the 11th day of Christmas, my true love sent to me:

Eleven pipers piping,

Ten Lords-a-leaping,

Nine ladies leaping,

Eight maids a-milking,

Seven swans-a-swimming,

Six geese-a-laying,

FIVE golden rings,

Four calling birds,

Three French hens,

Two turtle doves, and a

"A Partridge in a Pear Tree."

Narrator: Peter would later become the first pope and after him an uninterrupted lineage of other popes would follow, like the monarchy, like that of King Henry VIII, through a male heir. The eleven apostles chose his replacement. It was Matthias. It had to be a person who knew Jesus personally.

"We are finally at the end," cheers one.

"Twelve, the Apostles Creed," celebrates the other. "The creed has twelve parts, because it was written by the twelve apostles when Matthias joined. As there were twelve tribes of Israel, Jesus had chosen twelve apostles. St. Peter had to choose an apostle to replace Judas of Iscariot, who had taken his life. Matthias knew Jesus personally, and so he became the replacement."

"Let us use drummers," excitedly suggests one. "Twelve drummers drumming will sit in for the Apostle's Creed. Another easy one to celebrate."

"Easy reference," exclaims one, reaching for his notes.

I believe in God,

the Father almighty,

Creator of heaven and earth,

and in Jesus Christ, his only Son, our Lord,

who was conceived by the Holy Spirit,

born of the Virgin Mary,

suffered under Pontius Pilate,

was crucified, died and was buried;

he descended into hell;

on the third day he rose again from the dead;

he ascended into heaven,

and is seated at the right hand of God the Father almighty;

from there he will come to judge the living and the dead.

I believe in the Holy Spirit,

the holy catholic Church,

the communion of saints,

the forgiveness of sins,

the resurrection of the body,

and life everlasting.

Amen.

On the 12th day of Christmas, my true love sent to me:

Twelve drummers drumming,

Eleven pipers piping,

Ten Lords-a-leaping,

Nine ladies leaping,

Eight maids a-milking,

Seven swans-a-swimming,

Six geese-a-laying,

FIVE golden rings,

Four calling birds,

Three French hens,

Two turtle doves, and a

"A Partridge in a Pear Tree."

I believe in God,
the Father almighty,
Creator of heaven and earth,
and in Jesus Christ, his only Son, our Lord,
who was conceived by the Holy Spirit,
born of the Virgin Mary,
suffered under Pontius Pilate,
was crucified, died and was buried;
he descended into hell;
on the third day he rose again
from the dead;
he ascended into heaven,
and is seated at the right hand
of God the Father almighty;
from there he will come to judge
the living and the dead.
I believe in the Holy Spirit,
the holy catholic Church,
the communion of saints,
the forgiveness of sins,
the resurrection of the body,
and life everlasting.
Amen.

"Fantastic! We are done!"

They celebrate, "Very clever. It is rhythmic and fun. It hits the main points."

"Although divided, the song will live on, the doctrines will endure, the Church will persist."

Narrator:

For now, we are to recur to the

partridge in a pear tree and

the two books of the Bible, develop

the three theological virtues from

the four gospels and

the five books of the Torah; bask in

the six days of creation,

implore for the seven gifts of the Holy Spirit;

apply the eight beatitudes,

exercise the nine fruits of the Holy Spirit,

obey the Ten Commandments,

through the examples of the eleven disciples, (plus 1) and

attest to the Apostles Creed.

The End

Printed in the United States
by Baker & Taylor Publisher Services